It Was the Night of Christmas

ISBN 979-8-89345-446-8 (paperback)
ISBN 979-8-89428-042-4 (hardcover)
ISBN 979-8-89345-447-5 (digital)

Copyright © 2024 by Shaun E. Pitts

All rights reserved. No part of this publication may be reproduced, distributed, or transmitted in any form or by any means, including photocopying, recording, or other electronic or mechanical methods without the prior written permission of the publisher. For permission requests, solicit the publisher via the address below.

Christian Faith Publishing
832 Park Avenue
Meadville, PA 16335
www.christianfaithpublishing.com

Printed in the United States of America

It Was the Night of Christmas

Shaun E. Pitts

It was the night of Christmas,
and Jesus was in route,
The sheep in the pasture,
the shepherds watching out.
The angels were preparing to take to the air,
Because they had advance notice,
Jesus would soon be there.

The inns were all full,
nowhere to lay His head,
The animals moved around,
to make room for His bed.
While Mary sat down,
her stomach in her lap,
Joseph tore rags, for baby
Jesus to be wrapped.

Do not be afraid.

When the angel of the Lord appeared,
the shepherds started to scatter,
But the angel said, "Don't be afraid,"
then explained the matter.

The news of the Savior made a big splash,
Then a multitude of angels lit up like a great flash.
At the end of the announcement,
the shepherds were in the know.
The angels returned to heaven,
and the shepherds said to each other, "Let's go."

To Bethlehem they went,
having shed their fears,
To witness with their eyes
what they heard with their ears.

When the shepherds arrived,
there was no mortar or bricks,
Just Joseph, Mary, and the babe in a manger
filled with straw and sticks.

Now when the shepherds saw Him,
they went to proclaim
The good news about Christ the Savior,
but never mentioned His name.
The scriptures refer to Him as Immanuel,
Lamb of God, Alpha and Omega,
the beginning and the end,
To call him anything less would be committing a sin.

The shepherds completed their mission,
they answered God's call,
And they returned praising God,
for letting them take part in it all

Like time, when you're having fun,
news sure does fly
Now, the wise men from the East
saw His star in the sky.

They inquired about Him in Jerusalem,
to see if anyone knew
Of the one they came to worship,
King of the Jews.
King Herod was troubled, about
this king of the Jews,
So he said, "Tell me if you find Him,
I want to worship Him too,"
But deep down inside,
he was not telling the truth.

After listening to the king,
they all turned around,
And the star reappeared and
led them to town.

When they got to the house,
Mary with her child, there she stood.
They fell down and worshiped Him,
like they said they would.
When they stood to their feet
and opened their sack,
Their gifts of gold, frankincense,
and myrrh were still intact.

When they fell asleep, they were awakened
by a dream that seemed scary,
But it was God saying, "Don't go back to Herod,
go back to your own country, and do not tarry."

This is what happened on that one famous night.
Merry Christmas from Jesus, and to
all who believe eternal life!

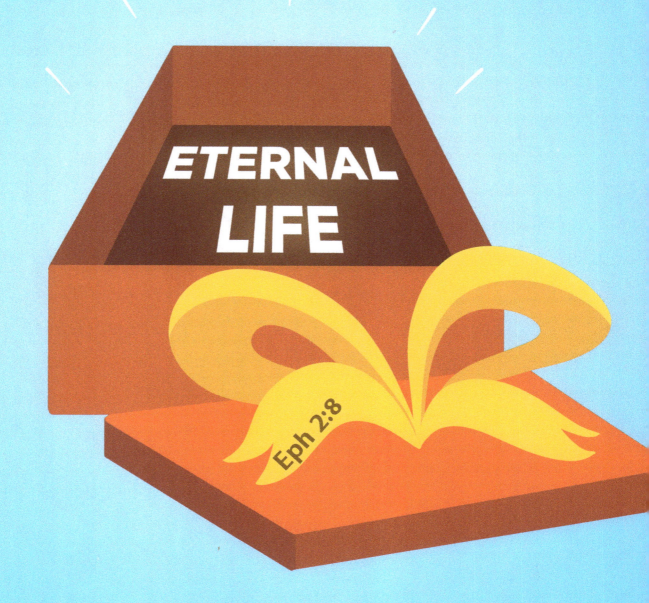

About the Author

Shaun E. Pitts is the pastor and founder of Ekklesia Bible Fellowship of Texas, a small local church committed to living out the Word of God in their daily lives.

Shaun is a graduate of Southern Bible Institute, where he received his BA in biblical studies.

Shaun believes deeply in family! He was born in Chicago, Illinois, and moved to Saint Maurice, Louisiana, where he met his loving wife, Fredia, of thirty-six years. They currently reside in Richardson, Texas, where they are surrounded by their two boys, DeShaun and Scott; two nieces/daughters, Sheniqua and Taylor; sister-in-law, Deetrice; and eleven grandchildren, Neihmiah, Jayden, Madison, Morgan, Jrue, Makayla, Chrissy, Landon, Kamdyn, Greyson, Jayce; and Shaun's mom, Maggie.

www.ingramcontent.com/pod-product-compliance
Lightning Source LLC
LaVergne TN
LVHW060738271224
799921LV00030B/1075